ZOO

By the same author:

ZOO

Tobias Hill

Oxford   New York

OXFORD UNIVERSITY PRESS

1998

Oxford University Press, Great Clarendon Street, Oxford OX2 6DP

Oxford New York

Athens Auckland Bangkok Bogotá Buenos Aires Calcutta
Cape Town Chennai Dar es Salaam Delhi Florence Hong Kong Istanbul
Karachi Kuala Lumpur Madrid Melbourne Mexico City Mumbai
Nairobi Paris São Paulo Singapore Taipei Tokyo Toronto Warsaw

and associated companies in Berlin Ibadan

Oxford is a registered trade mark of Oxford University Press

© Tobias Hill 1998

The moral rights of the author have been asserted

First published in Oxford Poets
as an Oxford University Press paperback 1998

British Library Cataloguing in Publication Data

Data available

Library of Congress Cataloging in Publication Data

Hill, Tobias, 1970–
Zoo / Tobias Hill.
(Oxford Poets)
I. Title.   II. Series.
PR6058.I4516Z66   1998   821'.914—dc21   98–21430

ISBN 0-19-288102-7

1 3 5 7 9 10 8 6 4 2

Typeset by George Hammond Design
Printed in Great Britain by
Athenæum Press Ltd.
Gateshead, Tyne and Wear

For Hannah, with love

Acknowledgements

Acknowledgements are due to the editors of the following publications in which some of the poems in this collection first appeared: *Frogmore Papers, Independent on Sunday, London Magazine, London Review of Books, Northwords, New Statesman, Observer, Orbis, Poetry Review, Stand, Staple, The Sunday Times, Tabla, Verse.*

Three poems were carried by London buses in June 1997 and May–October 1998.

The author would like to thank St John's College, Cambridge and the Wingate Foundation, who supported this book with (respectively) the Harper–Wood Studentship in 1996 and a Wingate scholarship in 1997.

This year the author is the inaugural Poetry Society 'Poet for Zoos', based at London Zoo.

Contents

Magnolia Flowers

In the dark
lightbulbs are opening.

The cats are out
hunting for blackbirds
through the green earthwires
of long grasses.

The trees are slight.
They are weighed down with blackbirds
which drink the sound of water
out of white bowls.

The water is cold and sweet
with magnolia pollen.
The mouths of the blackbirds
burn with it
like fusewires.

The cats hunt what they can.
The sight of burning mouths,
the sound of spilt water.

Draining the Grand Union

It happens quite suddenly,
the engineers doing their work
in the way important work is always done,

with no one noticing, until they've gone
and the canal with them. Its cold green
miles emptied quietly

as a gutter is emptied of rain.
The Grand Union Canal
has been removed, and left behind

are the skeletons of bicycles—
without wheels, without rust—
and twenty years of traffic cones
swollen, sheltering mussel shells
and torn-up letters, and lost coins

blackened or green with oxygen.
In the suntrap of a shopping trolley
an eel has worked its muscle
into soft brown knots
and died under the eyes of children
who watch its eyes turn into moons.

Behind the ten-foot doors
of the lock gates,
canal from here to Manchester
waits to find its level,

forcing green water
through the hinged black wood,

exploring in slow sheets
down old beams and bitumen.
There is the sour smell
of sun below the waterline

where a small man in pink Marigolds
rummages in the mud's cupboards.
Behind his back
the canal waits. Drips

drops. And up above,
a pair of tan-black dogs
watch it all from the footbridge,

their long, simple heads
full of the smell and the bright
shine of undiscovered country.

Twelfth Night

It is a warm winter this year.
The snow comes down as rain
and in your father's house

butterflies hang from the walls.
Scraps of pearskin lacquer
laid thin
across the cold of windows
and the dark arms of furniture.

Open a door
and they shift and dither
with the odd ends of paperchains.

For twelve nights we have been drinking
warm alcohol. Your father talks
of snow leopards escaped from zoos.
Uncle Joe's Minty Balls.
Ice Fairs and the rising seas
and winter butterflies.

They have been salted away
in hard chrysalids
the shape of green almonds

and now they are cracked open,
the world outside is
closed down under the rain.

Nothing here is meant for them.
A radio in the next room,
half tuned in. A pendulum

drowsing. Your father talking
of last June
in his whisky voice.
The way light fell between two bridges
on the Grand Union Canal,

wedged into the green surface.
As if the softness of light
and the density of water
had altered quietly as weather,
green hardening into glass.

Sushi

In the small hours
we eat sushi with our fingers.
It is a cold night
outside, and traffic
lights up the ceiling

in passing. On your skin
is the smell
of sweet abalone,
sweat, and ark shell, and bluefin.

You are picking
red salmon eggs
from white rice
carefully,
like a child with a chocolate biscuit.

On your palms
you warm the eggs,
their soft red pearls.

You break them open—
their skins are so tender—
with the tip of your tongue.

It is a warm night
and my heart is skipping
along, skipping
along—

I would kiss you,
but this is a time to remember
and first I will watch you

eating, and your grin
quick in the dark. I'm getting it clear,

so when I cast my mind back here
it will come skipping,
like a flat stone across flat water.

Michael the Zoo Keeper

His mother was a magician at nights,
pulling rabbits from a *Christy's* hat
after day shifts at Lillywhites,

Crouch End. For breakfasts, she cooked
dove egg omelettes.
He misses their paleness

in missing her. Cleaning cages
and the cells of the elephants
he remembers
the feel of her rabbit hat,
the fur felt
fine as the hands of night mammals,

fine as the hands of the dying.
It is past autumn, and in daylight
the gutters are still filled with the old
seeds of plane trees,
yellow as lionskin.

Now it is darker
and the zoo trees are bare.
Starlings glitter
in their hollow networks.

Darkness concentrates the senses.
Walking home, Michael
smells animals on his skin.
The sweat of the oryx
and the dry eyes of vultures

carried out with him, over
the tarred black water
of the Grand Union Canal
into the city streets

like contraband. Like magic charms.
A monkey paw, a rabbit's foot.
Cheap magic. The moon is out
and pale as a dove egg

to light him home.
He wraps his thin hands
round sweet tea and hot china

then lies awake, listening
for the wolves in their long cages,
for the chirr
of locusts in the reptile house,

all that is close and familiar.
He falls asleep before
the bored cough of a jaguar
echoes down Haven Street.

In the morning
there is snow falling
as he tunes through radio static,
waiting for first light.

The Elephant Girl

1

She forgets her own smell. She tries and can't
catch it. It is the way that she loses
the faces of friends, the streets of places.
Her hair and skin reek of rank elephant.

For sugar, Eve and Martha will fall down
like earthworks in the man-roar of the ring.
Their skin is grey and rough as pumice stone.
It chafes her fishnet thighs. She is smiling.

Two shows a night, and afterwards the tent
tugs and vents the wind over east London
and the elephant cells. Their tusks are gone.
Cut out. If they chose, nothing could prevent

the sum of their grey force. They are holed bones
in Moore's bronzes. The seamed mass of oceans.

2

   She thinks them patchwork—
love handles. The soles of feet.
   Nubs of fingerprints.

3

She dreams of chess.
The lathed pieces

turn under her horned palms
into the figures of new games.

Worked fossils of mice.
White frogs. The volutes
of seashells.

If she tries
she knows the rules
for the icons of lambs
and the movement of elephants.

The squares stink
of circuses. Small cells.
Butane. Adrenaline

and loss. Over this, hands move.
Touch-move.
The black rooks look like
bareback girls

and the horse totems
whisper, then couple themselves.

Closing Time

For ten days there is no weather
but fog. The air

pressed
into white slabs of mist.
I go for late night milk

out into the thick of it,
my ears ringing with the cold,
taking small breaths

and small footsteps. The roads
have lost their lengths and breadths

in cells of fog, and the pavements
are sluiced down with it,
dark as riverbeds.

The all-night shop is open,
its plaque of light
falling into the empty street

and I buy milk and greenback bacon
and walk home along the green
underpass of the canal.
My hands full
inside each cool pocket.

This is waiting weather.
The moon and the cars
go with slow care
through nothing towards nowhere

and home is further than I thought.
I put the milk
down on the black pavement,
feeling in the white dark
for the edge of keys

and south of here, the Zoo klaxon
begins to sound. Hours late
for closing time. The cry of it looming

through the enclosures of fog,
between the empty aviaries
of the ravens, and the ruined
tenements and alleyways

and the blue shark in its lit tank,
turning and turning back
without rest or impatience or surprise.

Leonardo's Machines

We're waiting for the light to change
and you are reading borrowed books.

The hinges of paperbacks
are held apart on your knees

and your hands
cradle the furred spines.
All day we have been arguing

about nothing. About each other.
Outside the birds are singing,

and the city lights already on.
You put Caesar's *The Civil War*
down by your feet,
with *How to Cook
a Wolf*. Open *Leonardo's Machines*,

turning the pages
as the light turns green.
There is Da Vinci's system
for walking on water
and his device for weighing air,

their line and shade
on smooth paper.
Page ten shows the facsimiles
of weapon forms derived from fruit.
xiv; the helmet-mask.
xvi; the oven-flower.

There is blood on my tongue
or just the taste of it.
There's nothing like the head-butt

of words, their thoughtful violence.
Now your hands are sleepwalking,
knuckles softening out

as the traffic crawls down Brewer Street.
Outside the door of GIRLS GIRLS GIRLS
waits a man in rabbit fur

worn thin, and a woman
in the warm brown leather
of her lover,

both faint in the faint light
as Leonardo's diagrams,

gorgeous and violent as dreams.
'If necessary,
I will build
mortars and light ordinance
with beautiful and useful shapes—'

the hand inventing,
in black chalk,
a way of drawing shadowed ice
or a foetus in the uterus.
The way of putting together
an oil-press. Machines of war

to end war. Moveable fountains.
A mechanical lion
with its chest opening
crammed with lilies—

'A will be young fir,
which has fibre
and is light. B will be fustian
and feathers. C will be starched taffeta
and for the trial you will use
thin paper—'

Your voice quiet. The car
louder. The sounds of you and it and us

not going far. Tonight
we won't make love or argument.
This is a quiet time. Look up and out.

Aeroplanes, sleek as guns,
are turning west into the light
and the air over the terraced streets
mutters at the miracle of flight.

Gibbons in a Northern Spring

Under the rain
the zoo enclosures
rust and drip
like shark cages.

The lions are awake,
smelling the reek of ibis
in the sieves of aviaries,

watching the plane trees
sodden and darken
in patterns of giraffe skin.

All day there is no sound but this,
the breath and boredom of lions
sullen as limestone,

the chirrup of traffic lights
turning green in empty streets,

and the gibbons
howling for a yellow noon
in their cages of rain.

How to Curse

1 *Ingredients*

Take time. Take out the brunt
force of *Jesus fucking cunt*.

For the cursing to go right
strip the mouth down to meat

and say nothing, and drink alone
on balconies, in waiting-rooms

that smell of hotplate coffee burnt
dry and sweet. Lick at your words, like salt.

Grin and your lips will split.
You come from the islands
where people do not lose their tempers;

they almost lose their tempers.
Lose nothing. Keep the lid down flat
on your own stinking pot.
Grin until you see the bone.

Save yourself. Choose your heart.
A pound of muscle laced with blood

works, or a lovebird in its cage
of ribs—what I mean to say is

hate with a lover's care and love
in company and absences.
To curse right, love your enemy.

2 *Fieldwork*

Look for violence
everywhere, and you'll find it
everywhere. In the chip-chop
echo of yards and building sites,

in the magpie who talks to the rock-drills,
    in the greenstick
    fracture
of sunlight through inches of glass.

In cities when the lights come on
and the starlings mass in flight,
settling and unsettling.
Their glitter and chatter. Hate can do that.

Wait on this seat in this public place
(where I remember her,
    where I remember her
    sweet talk and sweet small-talk—)

and look for studies in hatred.
There is a man who whispers
spittle and curses to the trees
which only listen, never talk,

which only breathe. And there is one
with her left hand in her right hand,
waiting for lovers, and finding

only the leaves around her,
welts of gold on the grey pavement.

She is waiting to find anything
to say. A greeting; a movement

of lips. Her fingers caged with hate.
Waiting to be promised something.

19

3 Curse

Promise me you won't forget,
and I'll promise something slight,

that all your journeys will be my journey
where no one stands waiting
at your stations

that all your homes will be my home
where the clock tick
seeds its age into your bones

Promise me you won't forget
and I'll promise what you'll get;

that looking for evening air
or space alone, or someone there
under the red night of cities,
windows and river-lights laid out
like cut stone on a jeweller's cloth—

all you will find is distances
a fear of falling,
a need to run. Only

I remember, you are leant laughing
at an open window
shooing away pigeons
that croo like lovemaking

remember I will still be here.
I promise I'll never forget
the deadbeat of your heart
in the dark,
the belling of your laughter there.
Remember that I won't forget
and you will always have my fear.

4 Breathing

When the cursing is all done
when the words are made and gone
don't go yet. Wait and sit

in the midpoint of the night
while the day and new day join
and the far coordinates

of the starlights gently turn
let the heat of hatred burn
out into the breathless space

sit in the heart's pause
while the moon loses its light
and the dawn is weak as thought

all around the rim of earth
softly sit and softly laugh
for the freedom and the dearth

where the hatred used to writhe
let the hatred be a wreath.

Close your eyes on all of this and breathe.

Flora & Fauna

Outside the station,
trees dense with green oranges.
I put down my case.

Birds try to settle
around the early streetlights.
I'm hungry for fish.

Monday, at first light:
the subway stairwell flooded
smooth for ten minutes

and wind underground.
I turn back for the reek
of human hair.

Drunk Autumn Midnight below Victoria Embankment

And the sky wet as a loose tarpaulin.
I'm walking but not home.

I'm taking the air. It tastes
sweet, like rust. The tide is out

and the mud is thick as meat
over the inner city's chalk.

Here are the broken fingerbones
of clay pipes. Traffic cones. The imprint

of my own feet, walking back.
Here is a seed stained black.

Live as a fist, but all I want
is somewhere to sit down a minute,

tomorrow's newspaper (the pages
hot with fish and vinegar)

and the watermark of London sky
green as old money all over the river.

The Patron Saint of Prisoners

There have been better years.
In late August, forest fires

eat through the locust trees,
the beehives burning in neat pyres

of sweet ash. When the meerschaum mine
lays off two hundred men,

The Oyu Zoo is ordered shut,
on grounds of luxury. The stepped

concrete of the wolves' enclosure
is earmarked for an outdoor theatre,

and the camel is auctioned off
in seven shares of fur and rough

topside. The aquarium stock
is given out in Oil Sellers' Park

to anyone who wants it.
Blue angel-fish and the white

ammonite curls of conch meat
spit and blurt in hot fat,

and the ostrich from the aviary
lasts until St Leonard's day

in November—the patron saint
of prisoners and fruit markets.
In the winter streets,

rabbit fat is cheap,
and cardamon and sugar beet

sell at the price of better things,
the town sick of the taste of meat.

Prospero's Cell

The whorehouses and warehouses
of munificent Milan
ring with cash and industry
behind their locks and doors.

In the Street of the Land of the Flies
and the Street of the Lamb
loiterers unlock hard grins

of gold (and gold is hard as trade)
to drink to him, the Exiled Duke,
under a sky
broken with flags.

They don't care that the freelancers still talk
of heresies. A stave, a book.
Witches won't drown, and nor will Dukes
is what some say, or they say

At least he is a Christian,
the man exiled to thirst and sea-salt
guilt-marked by fulfilled punishment,
like Griglié, the demagogue,
who has no tongue to tell his lies.

—The feasts of saints are kept,
and trade by land and sea is good.
Better than good (they say his blood
is white with impotence, his feet
always naked, and all he says is *Where is my cell? Where
is my daughter?*)—

Hidden by laws and tapestries,
the Duke grows old. A little man,
salt skin and an artist's hands.

Nothing to do. Nothing to say
of city-states—of Burgundy,
ransomed by the Arabic
for twelve white falcons
brought from the islands of sea-ivory—

Nothing to him. His voice is
latitudes, distances,
empty aisles of libraries.
The stained light of Venetian glass
stains his face with what he sees—

He sees the retch of storms and words. The island
in itself. The ocean's plow and sow.
The talk of a daughter drowned by wind.
Something said there, not caught, and still to know.

Doctor Crippen in Love

After work he feeds the wolves
in Regent's Park. Keeping his gloves

buttoned, and his fingers clean.
Giraffes with swimming-pool skin

move through the tenements and trees.
One of the wolves has china eyes,

or so it sometimes seems to him. Keen
whites, and blue-glaze irises—

dollybird eyes. He keeps his sleeves
free of her teeth, and watches
until the late spring light is gone.
All of them understand themselves.

There is more time on Sunday,
when he will pay the entrance fee

for the Zoological Gardens
to watch Cuban solenodons
poisoning lizards, or to read
under the green roofs of the reptile house.

Then church. Seven rows in front,
a baby quacks and clucks
in the pale echo-chamber
of morning service.

It stares up at the high windows
where a pigeon is landing,
the grey fingers of its wings

bent back, the innards settling
inside the warmish cage of bones,
the fine sponge of its perfect marrow.

He could explain all that,
would have someone to listen,
if he could. All day is time to kill, and time

to think of love. He eats his tea alone
in Archway, then starts walking

home. Outside the dark shop windows
strings of laburnum flowers
catch the streetlight above him,
and in its lamp, the lightbulb stutters
and stuts like a geiger counter.

He looks up. Past the bulbs and flowers
glitter Sirius and Mars,

thin with smog. He starts to walk again.
He'd go a long way, to see perfect stars.

Lime Light

There is subsidence.
My father would have hated this,
the groan and the green slump
of the chainsaw's work.

Under the lime tree, white roots
inch their tips
into the sump
of spring rain.
The walls and weight of houses
sink into their white branches.

It's an ugly tree
and it always has been.
The bark is warted black
as London brick
and a bag from Safeways
fluts and pops in the maze
of cut-up logs, twigs and limbs.

Years ago, the trunk
split open with rot.
My father spent two days
painting it with treacle skins
of creosote. I'm also there,

watching from the kitchen door.
Small. The brush strokes
are spare. Out in the sun he grins,
half with pleasure,
half with effort.

Now the tree surgeons
rock at the stump,
twisting it out.
And it comes. A rotten tooth
already dead. Tall as a man

and heavier. Under the black
pocked skin of the lime

the wood is white
as roots. It is barely spring;

there's not much green
or right in this. The tree is gone.

The black hole waits
to be filled in,

and the rooms of the house
alter to what is left of us,
full of a new and unexpected light.

Poem for a North London Wedding

for Patrick & Anna

North London suits them
as they suit one another,
down to the ground and the hopscotch game
faint on the asphalt. Late-night laughter

between terraces built to last
in 1890. Shopfronts stacked

with armfuls of green sugar-canes,
thighs of yam, and figurines

of ginger. Ghetto blaster drivers
booming north past Whitehorn Flowers

('Bridal Bouquets at Short Notice')
and the Kapetanios
'We Buy the Best, We Sell
for Less' Fish Bar: all this
life and colour
suits them as they suit each other.
It is the end of April,

the season of weddings and rain.
Joe in Joe's Fags and Mags
talks about nothing all week

but Arsenal and Patrick
over the Sun and chocolate eggs
while old ladies and gentlemen

wait outside the corner shop
for Anna, leaning together
in arches of hot gossip.

It is almost summer. The weather
suits them as they suit each other.

Already the evenings are warmer.
In the small hours there is rain

and blackbirds blink awake and sing,
in love with the sound of water.

Snapshot of an Egotist

I'm the one with seven forks,
wisped hair, the bingo grin.

Behind me is a mass of knees,
fat and bone leant together

in a gloom of monotone.
I'm propped against trunks

like Brunel posed with giant chains
or Hemingway, leaning on tusks;

at ease. Hands loom, out of focus,
big as birds, but at my service.
I'm the one with all the forks.
I'm the one. There are voices

touching overhead,
talking and talking back,
senseless as the sound of rain.
This is what the grin says:

'I've got the forks. I've got the knees.
And that's enough. There's nothing else.'
Shutters click and when I laugh,
lilac blossom pops like popcorn.

Is this all my fault, or is
all this for me? I can't believe my luck.
I'm going to scream again.
This is the life. Give us a kiss.

Self-Portraits by Children

This is called Kevin.
It has two keels and two strings.
The head is hairless and fits on
like this. The torso is made of things
which smile. Not like Jack

in profile, Jack full-frontal.
The line pocked where the crayon broke.
In this mirror no one would smile
at no one. His tongue is a joke
drawn and drawn again and then crossed-out.

Jane has nine segments and a head
haired upwards like a coconut.
Clark has amoebic legs and Margaret
is a map of Trinidad—

the smell of crayon, the mirror propped
up on a table, and the thought:
this is my face or could be that. And this
is where my thinking goes. I choose
how many teeth and if I stare—

the hands aching and the face on paper
not going how the hands want it.
Already gone and done, and the mirror
flat and obvious compared with Amber

who has seven sunflowers
instead of hands, or John-Luke
crumpled up without a face. Or Kate,

who is almost nothing,
a trajectory of ink.
Just something going somewhere.

Saturday Night Fever

Working the clubface
she is flash as fish skin

      she is teeth bared and head down
      deep in the limelights

and then outside, her winter coat
begins to smell of rain
suddenly, as if the sense
has been waiting there, quietly. The streets

      go on ahead of her, net curtains
          faded to the watermark
          of yesterday's light.

She could watch them for hours,
the rows of window ornaments
which lie like advertisements
for the rictus of porcelain,

for airless evenings and nights
inside her watchful family. The knives
of silences,   the little knives
of secrets hidden and sought out.

The hide-and-seek, ready or not. *Forty-eight,
forty-nine, a hundred.* Sloughs of butterflies
trapped without understanding
in the summer house's oven.
She hides among them as she waits

to be found out. Fingers their dust,
white and allergic to the light.

Their wings are thin
as Christmas glass.
She makes her face up with their dead pollen.

Down Camden Road at midnight,
a mother's voice calling to church,

              and the breath of the girl.
              Running, running.

A Night in the Room of the Clown

All night, the smell of greasepaint
rises from a circus-ring of rugs,
the leg of a sheepskin laid out
on the creased hand of a leopardskin.

I am waiting to sleep
on the chair, at the desk
with its one drawer missing like a tooth.
Alone in the room with my shoes on.
Tented with light
from a window of street
I go through papers, looking for facts.

Like a taxman. Here's a shot
of The Great Geronimo
lookout-poised at London Zoo.
Face washed white, except
for the pelt-holes
of his small eyes and big mouth.

I pick up jokes, put them back:
juggling balls. Rubber milk
and a cut-throat, smiling out
clean from its iron backbone.

There is the ordinary sound
of voices, calling voices home
outside, and a cement truck's groan
at a rabbit's skull,
the leer of its nudity
on the headlit windowsill.

If I click on the light, skins and bones
grin at the captive audience
of themselves. I sit alone,
laughing until it hurts
at the joke of growing thin,
the tick of the clock and the clapping of rain.

Excerpts from a London Zoo Guide Book, 1928

The Zoological Gardens
are most conveniently reached
by taxi. Bears like carrots
and especially anything sweet
such as honey, golden syrup
or sweetened, condensed milk.
Learning the animals' names will make them

attentive. Keep hold of possessions.
Avoid the bear-pit when it rains.
The dark-room is in the charge of the keeper
of the Wolves Den, and a coati is amusing
if given scent
on a small wisp
of cotton-wool.

Just here is the Aquarium
with its elaborate system of water
held in suspended reservoirs.
The tanks are lighted while the corridors are dark.

The white cobra is probably unique.
The building by the aviary
was erected for a 'sacred' white elephant
and its attendants. Most of them will beg
for food and some sit up
in very amusing attitudes.

Note the cage with radiant heat
where the lowest mammals may be seen,
the creatures which are fed at dusk,
anteaters and agoutis.

We have now reached the extreme
where tunnels and canal-bridges
lead out. Underground Railways
run on into the evening;
See Maskelyne's Mysteries
(c.v.), the Music Halls and Cabarets.

The Island of Pumpkins

In the hills of the Island of Pumpkins
I go walking.
The sun burns
my white skin. I am carrying

mixed currencies. A business card.
A bag of cold blood-oranges
bought cheap on the mainland.

Here
it is the seventh week of drought
since the end of the season of rain.

Around my feet are pumpkin vines
making yokes and watchsprings,
    searching for water
        in the yellow dust.

It has taken all night to get here,
and that with good transport
and now there's nothing left to see
but the easternmost hills
of an easternmost island,

their green bowls cupped
against green bowls

and a tractor leant sideways,
catching the sun
in its broken glasshouse.

Sound is slow to come this far,
carried and dropped and then picked back
up over the fields of pumpkins—
laughter, a joke. A foreign language
with no words for *miss*.
I miss

a tongue where I am not run dry.
Here I am surface-muck.
I miss place-names familiar as salt
and the dialect of rush-hours—

a klaxon hoots
                 drawn out
from the docks. There is the clank

of men unloading greenhouse glass
and blocks of ice in plastic green
as pumpkin skin wiped damp and clean—
and what I see is what I miss;

watching late trains cross
the bridge, the river. Years of rain
fallen down into the Thames.
Night falling on the homes and the homeless.

Dowsing with Whalebones

I am a follower of water.
If I stand at this junction of roads

I can divine its sound,
the bell and dirge of water

underground. The level, bubbled skin
and always the one direction.

I arrived here with the night train,
the smell of its engines and dust

a foreign language. This is the city
of dry cisterns. People sip

small measures in the bars, and grin
at intelligences of rain,
the force of it cracking their lips.

There is hopelessness in dry directions.
I get lost between the Street of the Flies

and the Street of Five Stations.
Left and right are inside of me,
compass-points are not—hopeless!

When I turn in the Square of Pigeons
my left eye is still my left eye
which was my north,
and is my south.

But these are my whalebones,
light and suppple as the seethe of plankton.
I follow them to troughs and gutters
and square miles of sewer pipes

because each city has its heart
and every heart is water. Here

is the gourd-thump of an empty butt,
here is the tock of grit in wells and sumps.

Down at the end of terraces
I find the source. The tide is out

and the light flat as mud.

I sit by the embankment
on the warm stone, and take the air,

having all that I came here for:
a souvenir of pigeon feathers
the colour of magnet

and the way home, which is straightforward
as downpour,

and a bed for the night,
sweet in the morning
with the smell of the river.

A Page of a Guide to a Small Island

The island cisterns have been dry
since the war. Eat moist fruits

and walk in shade. Buy currency
in small amounts.
The cost of living is not high.

Watch out for false surcharges,
the price of meat out of season
and the slight oracles
of a thumb's imprint in Roman pottery,
of a moth's wings
marked with road maps
and old sea lanes

Go walking through the old town,
where the stepped streets
smell of the thighs of pigs
and rotting cryptomeria—
but sunstroke can be dangerous.
Look out for warning signs:
burnt skin, slight dizziness, small voices,
the guttural vowel of water,

the struck stone
of a bat's tongue,
gauging distances.

There are new hotels each season,
more pleasure boats, less secrecy.
But do not underestimate
the strength of myth in an island state;

what has been lost was never strong—
the cracked urns
where bees hived, the muttering
and comb moulded
to one round lip. And
some things must be lost, while some things

stay for good. Sea caves hung
with looms of stone,
unfinished works of amethyst,

or the navigator's middle daughter,
waves slopped open beside her,
threading the hips of a bee.

Knotting it tight. It groans and turns
above her laughter.
Later, she'll take its wings away
and watch it roll in the summer dust
like the pigs.
Like an animal.

A Crossroads

1 *Walking in July*

I leave with no reason except to walk,
under the road trees, which are still and black

as wet concrete. Turn left and left and right.
This street is smoothed out new and flat

with curds and slatherings of tar,
hot through my shoes. This suntrapped square

has no name on the map. Two car alarms
panic together over rented rooms.

This is a place never meant for A-Zs or visitors:
lost space. No Dogs No Ballgames Squares

where no one hears the trees
fall and rise in their own branches.

Down here there is the sound of talk
in eyehole doorways and carpeted halls,
enquiries to help
with Missing Persons, Lost and Found.

There is the smoker's cough of police lines,
and echoed down between the flats
of Ratcliff, Ruthven, Ravenscar,
Martha's Soft Ice
Mind the Children
plays the ice-cream song.

Cold names. Officers come and go,
searching for joyriders, blip boys,
lift surfers. Pensioners shaking
their heads, shaking. 'I don't know him.'
'Not him. I have trouble with names.'
Grey skin on them, as warm and grey
as the hearts of artichokes.

As sweet as that. *Names trouble me.*
One hand moves on the public clock, or
all the hands move on all the clocks,

out through mapped streets and postal codes
and if I stand just here, just right

and look up, I can see the rain
coming, and light on aeroplanes
high and nameless, crossing time–zones.

2 *Last train, November 1st*

Out to the bedroom-towns with their
lurch of headlights over sleeping policemen

goes the twelve-ten with half-empty seats
smelling of cigarettes and factories.

This is the dark between stations where
nobody talks to no one, and the river

looms like a high-rise
under piers and viaducts.

In the night train's public places
we are the photofit faces

watching closing-times and derelicts
out of windows puzzled with rain.

In transit nothing counts. It makes us
full of possibilities:

some of us dream of rush-hours,
some of us will be dangerous.
This is what we come to when

the overtime is gone and there is
nothing left to do but listen
for public announcements or aggression—

the voice into a cordless phone
that lies like a dentist to its loved one,

the movement of air
in tunnels and wires,

the track, which says
I am correct—
I am the click of binary
in satellite and sea-bed lines,
I am the atom in the clock,
I am the metric length of gold.
It could be you. It could be you. It could
—and from the yards outside,

gently, the hush of a city and a river,
and the smell of rain coming in
through open doors at platforms and destinations.

3 *Shore leave in winter*

Waiting for thaw in a thin country
there is small-talk and small questions.

Why here. Where from. He always tells them
how he never learned to read.
It sounds like truth and is

part truth. There were other ways to own
the shape of the road-sign of his first town.

One letter was crossed like fingers.
He copies it out on the glass of his pint.
The last letter was crossed like a heart,

a printer's symbol of the heart,
its four-valved crossroad.
That was the word

for what was always promised,
home, spelt out black on white

like the brunt sea
under spilt foam.
The last sign out by the McClean farm.

There have been other ways
to read, without the thick silt
of last names and signatures.

The hatchworked script
of ice on a ship's glass,

meaning *North*, the mouthings of trawled tons
of scad and skate. The trick of reading stars

through clouds,
the lucidity of air
over distant water

and then the water,
which accepts any writing
like paper, only disturbed by tides.

But for now there is only lights out,
shut doors, the chuff of feet,

his feet, and the cold of the rain
falling down over Warren Street.

4 *Spring on the Underground*

After the alarm,
she lies back in her cold spring room
taking little sips of sleep
while sunlight spills across the floor.

Inside her was a dream
of rain lessening
in a dry country:
Pines smouldered and

needles shone, dark as pepperskins.
There was the pain of being touched
and the pain of almost being touched
in a locked room, in a locked room.

Now there is the northern city
of plane trees and mackerel skies.
The sun is in;
it looks like rain. Inside the Underground

is writing she can't understand.
LOVE IS GOØD. YIDS GO HOME.
SKREWDRIVER RULES. *The alien*

should tear along the perforated strip.
She waits in offices
with her left hand warm in her right hand.
Her ticket is shaped like a tooth.

There are forms to be understood,
words to be learned: *regime. Torture.*
Period of stay. She waits. Looks out:

small children are waving
through glass at their mother
who waits without seeing.
The bows in their hair
are shaped like kisses,
small kisses placed on foreheads.
She understands something of this.

She wishes for water's amnesia,
its magic hoops and puzzle-rings
vanishing over stones
and the impressions of rain.

Her ticket number's next. She stands,
looks out again. The roads are gone
into grey downpour.

She envies that deliverance.

The Sound of Cages

We walk each other home
eating takeaway food.

Licking the guttered mustard
from the warm bones
of wrists and hands. The lit

plinths of Docklands
are behind us, and across the park
comes the sound of zoo cages,

the crash of big animals
moving against small walls.
Cages leave nothing except time
to think, and nothing else to think

except that all cages have holes.
At nights, two escaped eagle owls
hunt our tenemented blocks

from the grey cupolas of St Paul's
to the falafel stalls of Camden.

Tall as children,
their cries bring me awake

without understanding. I listen
with my eyes open.

There is the sound of fire engines
across postcodes, and sometimes
soft voices at corners,
quiet as an ambush, and sometimes

a whistling in the dark,
cold and at ease in the stone
streets. Whistling home
with meat, and without quarantine.

The Pilot in Winter

*(In a remote coastal town to the south-west of Corinth is
the grave-site of Norman Mackay. In accordance with
Greek Christian Orthodoxy, his bones have been dug up,
washed with wine, and laid in a box the length of his
thigh-bone. The townspeople believe Mackay dropped the
atom bomb on Hiroshima from the B29 'Enola Gay' on
the morning of August 6th, 1945. There is no record of a
Norman Mackay on flight-crew logs for that exercise. The
population of the coastal town in winter is 300).*

I

Salt fruit on a white plate.
Yorgos the waiter takes and eats
handfuls of green olives. Spits out
the stones. Outside is the noon sun
and all the young waitresses.
He watches as they hang
octopus on coathangers;

stretched-out stars, and pink
as knickers on a washing line
and at the crusted ventilation slit
Yorgos smiles at the thought
with his eyes. It is clear weather
today, and the coast road
shimmers with its smell
of hot tar and last winter's rain

and in a while the melon man
will drive in past the old town,
on the new road,
with his cargo of green skin.

So Yorgos waits for him
and while he waits he cleans his hands
washes his forearms knuckle-white.

Opens the window. Leans out,
looking uphill to the old town
where the Pilot is, and the blood relations
in good boxes, washed in wine.

His hands smell of their bone.
He dries the skin and nails. Goes back out
into the hot light,
feeling for coins in his pocket,
shouting a price to the melon man.

II

I walk to the hills where the old town is,
and the old church with its twelve framed
Elijahs. Wheels and chariots of fire
leaved with bright tin and sweet dust.

Outside is the industry of bees
and the clink of goats. Hills away.
Sound carries easily up here

in the summer, when there is no rain
and the bone-shed door
natters when the bolt is drawn
from the outside, and I go in.

This is a dry place to come,
but cool. The air soured by wine
and the ground darkened with oil
around the doorway's light.

Here are the town's blood relatives,
who have all met,
who can be singled out
by snapshots on boxwood,
and the measurements of thigh-bone;
great-grandparents stacked up like olive crates.

The pilot's bones are stained with earth
to the colour of earth, and the skull
is turned back into the plough
of leg and rib. No lock, only
the shift of little bones
in the box as the lid is shut.

MAKI NOPMAN in chalky script.
Here there is nothing else, except
box, name and bones, and the sound
of trees shambling in the wind
from here to Corinth. Lines of high ground

silver and black with saltless fruit
over dead towns and city-states
and bloody stories, and blood guilts.

I bolt the door shut. A truck groans
down on the coastal road,
changing gears, miles away.
Overhead, fighter planes
catch the light, turning inland.

III

Under the tin roof he listens
to the seven months of winter rain.

His head hurts with listening
in the dark of his room
which is white in summer
but blue in winter
with damp and shadow

and because the rain
has fallen for so long
he can smell nothing,

as if the hills with their dust
goat-shit and balsam
and the rock-shore with its rind of salt

have gone. As if he is gouged out.
He dreams of drowning
with eyes open
under the white cages of rain.

6 a.m. By the coastal road,
the pilot stands outside the bars
and under the clock-drip of trees,
telling his stories. The bomb

warm in the south-sea island sun.
Light on the city of canals,
Hiroshima, and the bomb-cloud
rising behind them like a blackout—

—all of his bloody secrets
and his bloody lies. It does him good,
the talk. He puts his head back to taste
rain through the tamarisks,

sour and clean. The petrol-station
is open, and the workers' bar.
The rest is shut. He wipes his mouth,
feeling for words, and goes inside.

Nightlight

Under the nightlight
the page is yellowing
with the clock tick,
turning back
to the colour of wood.

There is nothing to do with it
except to write
and if the writing is about nothing

then it is about nothing.
My mind is still sluiced clean
with the joy of it,
sluiced cold and clean.

Where am I in this? Right here,
lodged in the lungs and bones
of line and line.
Haven't you seen me yet?

I'm right here, touching it.
Against the paper's flat
my hand becomes
the wing of a bat
in the nightlight

the foreleg of a horse,
or what you want. The mole's claw.
Darker. The blood and knuckle-crack

of thought; the arch of fingers
amazed and quiet

pulling the pen
into its last curve

OXFORD POETS

Fleur Adcock

Moniza Alvi

Joseph Brodsky

Basil Bunting

Tessa Rose Chester

Daniela Crăsnaru

Greg Delanty

Michael Donaghy

Keith Douglas

Antony Dunn

D. J. Enright

Roy Fisher

Ida Affleck Graves

Ivor Gurney

Gwen Harwood

Anthony Hecht

Zbigniew Herbert

Tobias Hill

Thomas Kinsella

Brad Leithauser

Jamie McKendrick

Sean O'Brien

Alice Oswald

Peter Porter

Craig Raine

Zsuzsa Rakovszky

Christopher Reid

Stephen Romer

Eva Salzman

Carole Satyamurti

Peter Scupham

Jo Shapcott

Penelope Shuttle

Goran Simić

Anne Stevenson

George Szirtes

Grete Tartler

Edward Thomas

Charles Tomlinson

Marina Tsvetaeva

Chris Wallace-Crabbe

Hugo Williams